THE REALITY
OF
PROFESSIONAL
PET SITTING

ROTH

THE REALITY

OF

PROFESSIONAL
PET SITTING

*A Candid Look At
A Growing Profession*

SuZanne M. Roth

Library of Congress Number: 98-89466
ISBN#:   Hardcover   0-7388-0295-6
                  Softcover   0-7388-0296-4

This book was printed in the United States of America.

To order additional copies of this book, contact:
Xlibris Corporation
1-888-7-XLIBRIS
www.Xlibris.com
Orders@Xlibris.com

CONTENTS

DEDICATION

Whenever something funny, scary or unusual happens to me while on the job, my husband and I will always tell our friends and family about the incidents. We love how each time we tell our story, they look at us with wonder in their eyes. It is obvious that they are curious as to what possesses us to stay in the pet-sitting business. When I find them looking at me in that way, I always say "I know, I know, I could write a book!", and my husband always looks at me and says "As long as she's happy, I'm happy". In my heart I knew all along that someday I would write about my experiences, and that I would surely dedicate my book to him.

Therefore, this book is dedicated to my husband, Michael, because of his obvious love for me and his remarkable understanding of my love for animals. There are many other reasons that I have dedicated this book to him; as you read on, the other reasons will become increasingly evident!

This book is also dedicated in part to our baby, Shadow. He was 8 years old when I entered into this profession, and he wasn't happy that I did so. How do I know? Each time I'd come in the door after pet sitting, he would greet me as he always did…and then he'd turn his nose up and walk away. He was very jealous, knowing I had been in the presence of other animals! He was king of the house. In the midst of writing this book our beloved Shadow, who was with us for 16-1/2 years, left this world. He was our only baby, and we don't think our hearts will ever stop aching.

We love you, Shadow.

A PET SITTER'S DOG DAY...MORNING, AFTERNOON, AND NIGHT!

If you're having trouble sleeping, the experts say
"go to sleep and get up
at the same time every day".
For a pet sitter that's not so easy to do,
our calendars change drastically from day to day.
When you check your calendar at night,
you may have five different houses to visit
the next morning...or you may have only two.
So, the time you need to get up each day
depends on how many pets need care
the next morning—
for a sitter, that's the only way.
Rolling out of bed in the morning,
you stumble over your dog.
Looking at you with those sad eyes,
she's wondering how long you will be this time
(she knows your routine better than you).
You reassure her that you won't be long—
only an hour or two.
When you first get into pet sitting,
especially if you have only one pet
and even more so if your "baby" is a dog,

ROTH

they turn their nose up at you
and you swear they hate you.
After all, before it was "just you and me".
A pet sitter's own pets are masters
at making you feel guilty.
Not knowing that you're doing this
to put food in their dish—
they're wondering "why would she rather be
with other animals than be with me?".
How do you think your dog knows,
when before you come into the house
you change your clothes?
The answer to that puzzle is easy—
they know you've been around other animals
because "the nose knows"!

You venture out no matter what mother nature is
bestowing upon you, with instructions in hand,
driving here and there,
past land after land.
When your done feeding and walking all dogs,
and picking up all poohs, you stop
to get a cup of coffee, and read some news
in your favorite coffee shop.

It's not so easy to relax though,
since in a few hours
out again you'll need to go.
The afternoon will be here before you know it.
Depending on the number of pets you have that afternoon,
you start calculating
the time it'll take you to walk the dogs...
and feed the cats, birds, iguanas and rabbits!

SUZANNE M. ROTH

Meanwhile your dog is on your mind—you're thinking of how
   she's probably tapping her foot, patiently waiting.

As you gulp down your coffee,
you fold your newspaper
(you'll just read it later)—
not exactly what you had in mind.
You drive quickly to get home,
just to see that wagging behind!

In no time at all it's after noon,
your dog looks at you with those big, sad eyes again.
She knows you're leaving when you pick up your keys,
and you tell her "you won't be that long,
and soon it'll be her playtime again!".
When all the pets are taken care of and content,
you stop to get something for dinner.
You won't have time to cook, since you'll only have
an hour or two of quality time with your husband—
you'll need to go back out at night
to take care of Max, Lucie and Tigger.

All pets content and happy,
you arrive home late at night.
Your dog is waiting for you with ball in mouth—
it's playtime—she knows this very well—
to break the routine wouldn't be right.
She'd be very unhappy if you didn't spend
this quality time with her,
believe me—you'd be able to tell!
So with the yard lit up, you play and play,
until she's had enough—
she's probably already looking forward
to playtime the next day.

Finally, you can go in—can you really relax?
Not yet, there are some people
you need to call back.
You wonder if they would mind if you waited
to call them the next night—they probably would.
Oh, don't forget, you need to look at the next day's calendar…
Then you can finally read that newspaper!
Well, if your eyes would stay open you could.
Well, there's always tomorrow's news.
If you're having trouble sleeping, you know now what to do.
With a sitter's dog day mornings, afternoons, and nights—
having trouble sleeping
couldn't possibly be an issue!

SUZANNE M. ROTH

FOREWORD
BY THE AUTHOR

I am the Founder and Operator of NOAH'S ARK PET SERVICES. I have been a Professional Pet Sitter for the past eight (8) years. Many people do not know what a pet sitter does. In summary we take care of pets (while their owners are traveling for business or pleasure) in their own home, eliminating the need to transport them to a boarding facility. The pet owners' houses are also taken care of; e.g., mail/newspapers/flyers are taken in, alarms armed, lights adjusted, plants watered, etc. Most Professional Pet Sitters also offer daily walking services for corporate workers, who may need to travel by train or drive many miles to and from work—turning their "9 to 5" jobs into more like "7 to 7" jobs; these visits provide relief and exercise to the pet(s), and peace of mind to the pet owner. A pet sitter's primary duty is to provide services with a caring and professional style. Pet sitting has been a growing profession for more than 12 years now. However, when pet owners need to travel, most still automatically board their pets. Some are simply unaware that pet sitters exist. When pet owners finally do hear of pet sitters, many are thrilled that there is an option to boarding their pet(s).

So, you want to learn more about this captivating profession. The reasons for your interest could be one of several. Perhaps you consider yourself to be an animal loving, self—motivated, determined, reliable, trustworthy, dependable, punctual, patient, persistent, energetic, personable individual, and are interested in becoming a Professional Pet Sitter. Perhaps you presently use the services of a Professional Pet Sitter. Perhaps you have never heard about pet sitting before you saw this book, and are curious to learn more about it. Whatever the reason(s) for your interest, this book will be "eye opening" and is a very enlightening look into the world of pet sitting. It has been written mainly for anyone who is considering pet sitting as a profession. It will help potential pet sitters determine whether or not in-home pet sitting is something they should pursue. (It should definitely be read before printing up those business cards!)

Just imagine (as you read on, I am sure you will wonder if these incidents are fictional or fabricated)…

CHAPTER 1

A Unique New Year's Eve Celebration

You are called to take care of 2 Sheepdogs—you have your first job! However, your husband asks you not to take it. Why? Besides the fact that it's New Year's Eve, the house is 12 miles away, which means you won't make any money. (You don't charge to pick up keys; therefore, by the time you drive there to get the key, drive home, then do the actual job and drive home, you've now driven 48 miles.) But you are just getting into business, and if this is the way to start you're going to do it. Aside from the fact that it's New Year's Eve and the rest of the world is out celebrating, it's raining... "cats and dogs". Even though the yard is fenced, you are asked to walk the dogs on leashes "because they won't listen when you want them to come back in". You ask your husband (God bless him) to come with you, so he can walk one dog while you walk the other...after all, you want to be together no matter what you're doing on New Year's Eve. (Oh, it happens to be your birthday, too!) He is not too happy, but he agrees. So, there you both are, walking 2 dogs in a muddy, fenced yard, umbrellas in hand. You both must look pretty silly to the neighbors, having dogs on leashes in a fenced yard! You then imagine what the dogs would look like, if you let them run free in that mud—and you don't care what anybody thinks because *you* would need to get all that mud off of them! If you asked your husband, you are sure he could think of better ways to be celebrating!

CHAPTER 2

The Definition of Commitment

You get a call to take care of a tabby. Again, the customer is out of your area, but you agree to do the job. The cat needs shots—2 times per day. You have never administered shots, and are honest with the customer. Some pets with certain medical conditions need shots, just like some people do. The shots must be administered every 12 hours. The question comes into your mind "should I charge more money for administering shots?" The obvious answer at this point is "no" (you don't want to lose the customer). You go to meet the cat and the owner. You are shown how to give the shot. You do the first two visits—you are becoming a "pro". The cat is cooperating (which you find out later is not usually the case). Then, an ice storm hits. It's a Saturday. You'd rather stay in bed like the rest of the world. It is so bad out that the Interstate highway near your house is closed. You *must* go out—you can't have anything happen to that cat while he's in your care. You are the only person crazy enough to venture out, except for the highway crews, police, and medical emergency vehicles. It takes you double the time to get there, not to mention the fact that you're risking your life—but you know you're doing what needs to be done. You know that the cat has a serious medical problem, and you will not have peace of mind if he doesn't get his medicine. This is also how you build a good reputation.

SUZANNE M. ROTH

CHAPTER 3

The Un-Cool Collie

You're walking a Collie three days a week—his owner is at work. He comes right out with you in winter—but in summer you have a problem. Like you, he doesn't like the heat. (You can understand why—you're hot and you don't have all that fur!) On one particular hot and humid day, you coax him outside. All he wants to do is go back into the air-conditioned apartment, which you wouldn't mind doing yourself. There are no trees to head for…you are walking, walking, walking the dog everywhere. He has to find just the right spot. If he doesn't "go", you know he will in the apartment by the time the owner gets home five or six hours later. Then, the owner will wonder what he's paying you for. Finally, success! You bring him back to the apartment. You look for the key on your ring of a thousand keys. Your panic attack begins— you can't find the key. (You meant to take the key off that flimsy ring the owner gave you, and put it on a more secure one…). You have to retrace, retrace, retrace your steps (did I mention it's the hottest day of the year?) Your blood pressure is rising right along with your body temperature. The dog doesn't want to walk fast, but you want to quickly find that key! You are talking to yourself, the dog, and God. You are searching, searching, searching everywhere. (If you never believed before this day that God exists, you start believing today.) You see a shiny object in the grass, after a very long and grueling half-hour search. (If you don't already have one, this will give you your first gray hair! I don't care how old you are, you will get at least one!) You get home and tell your husband what happened—he tells you to "go back to office work; you'll be cool in summer and warm in winter!".

SUZANNE M. ROTH

CHAPTER 4

"Caught Between a Rock and a Hard Place"

You have 2 indoor cats to take care of for a whole summer while the pet owners are at their vacation house. You go in one day—a mouse had found its way in, as well! It is in between both cats with nowhere to run! This is just your luck—did they have to notice the mouse while you were there? Couldn't they notice it during one of the other 23 hours in the day? (You think *you're* unlucky—imagine how the mouse feels!) You are witnessing this torturous deed, and there's nothing you can do; both cats aren't friendly—even to you—and you don't want to get too close to the mouse anyway! You feel sorry for it, but are afraid of it at the same time! You turn and walk away, knowing full well what is going to happen to that poor creature. You go about your business, holding your ears as often as you can, wondering if there will be any trace of that poor thing the next day. Of course, it's on your mind the rest of the day and night. The next day you find what's left of it right inside the front door. You can't just leave it there. You decide to pick up its remains with the fireplace shovel, trying not to look while you're doing it. (How impossible is this?? Try it sometime!) You are told by the customer when they get home that the reason they leave the cats at this house is so they'll catch the mice (which is fine, but did you have to see them catch it??!). From that day on, for 3 long months, you wonder every time you go into that house if you're going to step on a dead mouse.

CHAPTER 5

Mr. Squirrel's "Bee-reaving" Burial

Taking care of the same cats as in CHAPTER 4, you find Mr. Squirrel has fallen from the tree—right outside the front door! Of course, knowing you have to come back every day for the next 3 months, you don't want to leave him there. You can't bring yourself to pick him up (a tiny mouse is bad enough, but a squirrel…??!!) So, you take your poor husband with you the next day to dispose of him. He picks him up with a shovel. Then there's the dilemma of what to do with him (any animal lover knows that you can't just throw a dead animal in the trash!). You ask you husband to bury him alongside the driveway (it's a very wooded area). You are there with him, with your hands over your eyes. In the process he disturbs a bee nest—and they come swarming at both of you! You both run—your husband is right behind you with shovel in hand. You get to the car, and you both start laughing like crazy, imagining what the neighbors are thinking if they saw him running after you with a shovel!

CHAPTER 6

An "Alarming" Wake-Up Call

You are asleep after a long summer day (you are busiest in the summer—the whole world goes away at the same time!) You got in at 9:30 p.m. from your last dog walking. The phone rings—it's the alarm company for one of your clients. (This is included in your services. Customers leave your name with the alarm company when they are out of town.) You are told which client's alarm is blaring—and you need to go and re-set it. Of course, the customer will pay for an extra visit, but the house is 11 miles away in a secluded area (did I mention it's the middle of the night?) Of course, your husband, knowing where the house is, offers to come with you (if you're lucky!). Just as you suspected, the cats had set the alarm off. You call the alarm company, and they tell you how to re-set it.

CHAPTER 7

The Inaccessible House

You attempt to get into your customer's house to take care of their 3 cats. You only have the key to their front door. When leaving the house to go on their vacation, they went out the garage doors…and forgot their storm door is locked! Luckily, there is a screen in the door and not glass… you have no choice but to rip the screen to unlock the inside door. Of course, you can't leave the screen door like that, so you bring your husband the next day to fix the screen. (You're lucky if you have a husband who has mechanical abilities, *and* will put up with things like this!)

CHAPTER 8

"Life Can Turn on A...Key"

You are asked to take care of the same 2 sheepdogs as in CHAP-TER 1. You agree (you are a glutton for punishment!). This time, the key will not open the door. The customer is away on vacation for a week; therefore, you must find a way to get in. The dogs—and your reputation—are depending on it. You stand there for 10 minutes, praying that the lock is just stuck. You know this is the right key. You go around to the windows, hoping one was left unlocked. Then you realize that even if there is an unlocked window, the alarm is going to go off if you open it. Many of your customers tell you to hold onto their keys...you begin to doubt yourself...is this the right key? Again, your reputation is on the line. You must get in to care for those dogs. After several long, breath-free minutes, the key works. (If you still didn't believe in God before this incident, you definitely start believing in Him now!) When the customer returns, they tell you this happens once in a while...why don't they tell you these things *before* they leave??

CHAPTER 9

Learning a Lesson—the Hard Way

You normally take care of a Beagle on a daily basis while your customers are at work. They decide to go on vacation. You go in for your first visit, and you hear an all-too-familiar tone. You are all too aware of what that tone means! They went away, and forgot to give you their code—and you forgot, too! (They don't set the alarm when they are at work. There is nothing you can do. The alarm starts to blare. All you can do is sit there, while you heart pounds in your chest, and wait for the police. Calling the alarm company will do you no good—you don't know the password. The police come. A nervous wreck, you proceed to explain that you are supposed to be there. But, of course, they need proof and look at you as if you are a criminal until you provide it. You have learned a lesson, and will always be sure to ask if the alarm will be set, and what the code is!

CHAPTER 10

The Uncooperative Alarm

You sign up a new customer. They also have an alarm. You aren't worried though, because after the incident in CHAPTER 9, you know to ask about the alarm! You are given the code and the password. You can rest easy. You're still a little nervous the first day. You calmly push the code numbers…the alarm is not turning off. You know darn well that you are pushing the (!??!) numbers they gave you. Frantically, you keep pushing those same (!??!) numbers, knowing full well that there's something wrong and that any second now the alarm is going to start blaring. The inevitable happens. It is so loud, you can't hear yourself think. You're still pushing those buttons. Meanwhile, the phone is ringing—but you don't know it, because the alarm is so darn loud. It's the alarm company calling—they are waiting for you to answer and give them the "password". All of a sudden, the police are at the door. You find yourself explaining the situation, and feeling like a criminal again!

CHAPTER 11

No Living Thing

You are taking care of a German Shepherd on a daily basis while his owner is at work. You are told to feed the dog raw hamburger meat. You know in your heart that raw meat is good for no living thing; however, do you question what a customer is feeding his own dog? It is not your place to preach to him and tell him what he should or shouldn't feed his dog. Hesitating, you feed the dog the meat for a few days. Then one day, you take him out for his walk after feeding him, and he starts vomiting. Then, he gets diarrhea. He is so weak, he can barely stand up. Your worst fear has come true—he is sick from the meat. You call the owner at work. He begs you to take the dog to the vet. Of course, you will…you can't leave a dog with food poisoning all day long…food poisoning is life threatening. You get the dog to your truck (you need a 4-wheel drive truck for those freezing days when it's snowing—that's another story!). He's too weak to jump into the truck. You have to literally pick him up (he weighs a good 70 pounds). You take him to the vet. Of course, you're panicking because you have other visits scheduled, and you know you're going to be late. You also know you're going to have some messes to clean up when you finally get to them. You leave him with the doctor, and return later—only to be told they are keeping the dog overnight—he needs IV fluids. The vet confirms that the dog has food poisoning, and you can now tell the customer that "the *vet* said he shouldn't feed raw meat to the dog"…

CHAPTER 12

The Secret to a Hidden Personality

You are to take care of a large mixed-breed dog. He's okay when you go to meet him. The owner leaves for another state, leaving a note stating "by the way, Bear (you would think his name would have been a clue) is not walked on a leash. Just let him out the back door". You are just about to open the back door, when you realize there is no fence! You don't feel comfortable just letting the dog out...what if he runs away? Besides, it is your policy not to walk dogs without a leash. You go out to the car to get your spare leash. Big mistake. Your husband is waiting for you in the car this time (it's very early on Sunday morning, and you are going to go to breakfast after your visits, since you didn't have the time to eat before you left). You come back to the door with the leash...the dog sees it and goes bonkers, showing his teeth, jumping on the sliding storm door. You stand there in shock, hoping he will come to his senses and stop. He doesn't. He knocks the storm door off it's hinges! You have the door in your hands, you are holding him back with it. You feel the blood drain from your face...you are scared to death to say the least. This dog can do some damage. (By the way, you were told that the dog is afraid of men, so your husband can't get out of the car to help you. If the dog sees him, it will only add fuel to the fire.) You are standing there with the door in your hands. You look over at your husband, and he looks sympathetic—then he starts laughing! You really must be a funny sight. You can't just leave...you must go in. You say a prayer and yell "Bear, back!" as loud and deep as you can. (You never knew

ROTH

your voice could sound so deep and loud!) He backs off—proof again that God exists. When you get in the car, your husband reminds you that you have other skills. He also reminds you not to attempt to walk Bear with a leash again. You do not intend to walk him at all! You ask him if he didn't know the dog hated men, would he have come to help you...he tells you he's not that crazy!

You both found out today that you have more guts than either of you thought. He laughs every time he tells this story, and he tells it often.

SUZANNE M. ROTH

CHAPTER 13

The "Wedgie"

You are walking a Chow. He lives in an apartment building, and you have to walk him in a certain large wooded area. He is the type of dog that needs to find "the perfect spot", and likes to hide in tall grass or weeds. He's on a long, flexible leash, but you still have to walk through some woods. It's summer and you know there are plenty of ticks, fleas and poison ivy in those woods with you. The dog does the same thing every day. He darts deep into the woods, and then he darts out when he's done. One day, he attempts to dart out, and gets caught in a vine that's wrapped around a tree. The vine is now wrapped around his neck—he is wedged. There is no one around to ask for help. You begin to sweat…and curse. You have to go into those woods with God knows what in there with you to attempt to free the dog. You pull on the vine, trying to make the dog back out—he doesn't. His first instinct is to push forward, and he wedges himself even more. He knows he's stuck, he's panicking, and growling, because his air is being cut off, and you aren't getting him free fast enough. The only thing to do is start using a key to cut away at the vine. With much patience, sweat and many tears, you free him. Can it be that out of all those woods, this dog had to find that one spot to dart out from?

SUZANNE M. ROTH

CHAPTER 14

A Puppy—An Angel—A Miracle

You are taking care of a menagerie of pets, including 2 dogs. One of the dogs is a senior Beagle, and one is a very large, untrained, mixed-breed "puppy". The back yard is fenced, partly wooded, and goes up on a hill. You let the dogs out. You are in the house, preparing their food, as well as medication for the Beagle. When you call them to come in, only the Beagle comes. You don't see the "puppy" anywhere. You go into the yard (closing the door behind you, so the cats stays in). As you always do, you checked the gate before you let them out. You call his name, whistle, throw his ball…no dog. Panic setting in, you frantically climb the hill, looking behind every tree. You get this awful feeling the dog is not in the yard. But you still keep searching, because you don't want to believe that this is happening. After combing every inch of the yard, you face the facts—it's happening—he's gone. You lock up the house, and get in your car to search the area. You are praying for a miracle, and with a very busy highway nearby you are imagining the worst. In tears you return with no dog. As you pull into the driveway, you see what you believe is a vision from heaven—a little girl is standing there, holding the dog by his collar. You thank God again (and you now believe in angels). The little girl looks at you like you're insane. You can understand why—you probably look fright-ful, and you're certain your entire head has turned gray. You are cry-ing tears of joy now. With an angelic smile, she tells you "he does this a lot". Suddenly, the tears of joy stop—and you get angry. It would have been nice if the pet owners warned you that the dog likes to jump the fence! If you had known, you would have stayed outside with him, and this never would have happened.

SUZANNE M. ROTH

CHAPTER 15

The Fox {Terrier} Hunt

You are taking care of a Fox Terrier on a daily basis. Her name is Lucie. (You've given her the "pet" name of "Lucie-Belle". You've taken care of her for years now, with no problems. She has a fenced yard to run in. She's a very fast little dog, and has been known to catch rabbits and mice. (She has brought you several "presents" while taking care of her…) You are to never let her get out of the yard, because "she'd be a mile away before you noticed". One day you let her into the fenced yard. You're not worried, she's too little to jump over the fence, she's not a digger, and you already checked the gate. You are in the house, preparing her food. A couple of minutes go by, and you're waiting for her to come back to the door, as she always does, because she knows she's going to eat. You start getting "that" feeling again (only an experienced pet sitter knows this feeling). You rush out and call her. The gate, which is on the side of the house, blew open from the strong winds! The words "she'd be a mile away before you could even get in your car" are playing over and over in your head. She could be anywhere by this point. Having a full-blown panic attack, you start to hyperventilate. Should you stay at the house in case by some miracle she comes back…or should you drive around, knowing if you go one way, surely she's going the other way. You go out front, calling her name, and praying. The gray hairs are popping out. Leaving the gate open in case she comes back, you drive around the neighborhood. When you return, you realize that you must call the owners—you'll tell them exactly what happened and they'll understand. It wasn't your fault. As you dial, you know full well they won't understand—even if they say they do, you know that they won't really. This is a dog who is loved—a lot—and you were trusted to take care of her. As you are calling, you hear her collar jingling. You rush to the front door and you see her (another vision from heaven!) You've never been happier to see a dog in your life. You open the door, and she starts running again! She runs across the street. You are crying your eyes out (AGAIN!), having what you believe may be heart failure complete with shortness of breath, and you yell across the street to the homeowner, who is in her driveway, to please grab the dog. She doesn't even try to help. You start mumbling curse words you didn't even know you knew. You are calling the dog's name. She looks at you, and you run into the back yard, hoping she'll follow. Miraculously, she does! You close the gate, pick her up, and as you're bathing her with your tears you tell her never to do that again! Meanwhile, she's licking your face. You tell the owner later that night what had happened, adding that "Fox Terriers" are appropriately named, since their dog could definitely outrun a fox! They laugh and tell you it wasn't your fault…and that the woman across the street doesn't understand English…! You reach for a box of hair color…

SUZANNE M. ROTH

CHAPTER 16

Little Teeth Hurt, Too

You sign up a customer—they have a cat (who tries desperately to get out when you open the door), and a dog (who doesn't want to go out). You are told after you complete your form and are about to leave that it takes a while for the dog to warm up to a person; also, that he is not accustomed to being walked on a leash…you begin to see flashbacks from CHAPTER 12. You tell yourself that this is only a little guy, things can't turn out like that! You arrive for your first visit. The dog does not greet you at the door. Of course, the cat does. He would gladly go out! The dog is sitting on the sofa, and wants nothing to do with you. He doesn't budge, and is not about to. He is making large growling sounds, larger than you would expect from a small guy. You remind yourself, again, that he is just a small dog—how bad can those little teeth hurt? (A lot, the way they're always sharpening them on those bones!) You remind yourself that you're not supposed to show a dog that you're in the least bit intimidated—they can sense that. So you get closer, talking to him, as if he really cares what you're saying. He shows you a few more of his razor-sharp teeth, and you know he is not smiling. Suddenly, you realize those little teeth can hurt just as much as big teeth. You sit on the sofa, talking to him, trying to get closer. The closer you get, the louder he growls, and the more teeth he shows you. Finally, he gets down (you got a little too close), and you think you may be able to get the leash on him. Wishful thinking! He runs into the kitchen, and you follow him. You try giving him a treat—he doesn't want it. You try putting food in his bowl (maybe when he sees that you're feeding him, he'll warm up to you…yeah, right). You decide to leave him alone for a while, and try again later. It is now 9:00 p.m. You have already been there double the time, and haven't even gotten the dog outside for his walk yet. Meanwhile, you have 2 other houses to go to yet, and you know the dogs are probably crossing their legs by this time. Finally, you realize you must be brave and just leash the dog. The dog realizes he has no choice—he's probably too afraid to actually bite you. He walks to the door with you. He really hates you now, because he doesn't like leashes. You try to get him out, while keeping the cat inside (you can't put the cat in a room somewhere and shut him in—he won't let you pick him up—anyway, what if you forget to let him back out??!!) You finally get the dog outside. However, he will not "go"…because he's on a leash. Needless to say, you have poohs to clean up every day. Don't worry, things get better by the 8th visit…

CHAPTER 17

The Deception

You go to meet a dog and his owner. The dog is a male, full-grown boxer. You walk in and the dog is tied… inside the house…on a 5-foot leash! It breaks your heart to see a dog tied, especially inside a house. You begin to wonder why some people even have dogs; and if you really want to take care of this one. The owner can tell by your face that you are not thrilled about this situation, and he tells you he keeps the dog tied because he has small children, and he's afraid the dog will jump on them. He tells you that you will need to hook another leash on him, then take him off the leash that's bolted to the wall, and take him outside. You have bad feelings about this. You go for your first visit. The dog is growling at you, showing his pearly whites. (This dog has large teeth!) He is growling because he's afraid of you, and he "goes" all over the floor. Feeling sorry for the dog, you feel you should take him out anyway—you can't just leave him tied up for a whole week without some exercise. Shaking like a leaf, you get the strength to quickly hook him onto the other leash. After all, he's probably more afraid than you are. You know very well a scared dog will bite, if he gets the chance. You walk him, wondering if it'll be this way for the whole week…the dog warms up a little, and you give him as much love as you can. You make a promise to yourself that you will never be this naive again. The dog was tied, because he is being abused - not because he jumps. You are told when the owner gets home that he thinks the dog may have *been* abused before he got him—by a woman! (No wonder he hates you! If you're a man, you can go ahead and pet sit in this situation!) In my opinion this dog is still being abused.

You can't help thinking of another boxer you take care of ("Maverick") when his owner is away. That dog is treated the way every dog should be treated (especially boxers, who are very loyal dogs. . .with dignity and love).

CHAPTER 18

The Curious Beagle

You are to walk a Beagle on a daily basis. You give your regular rate. You go the first day, and you walk the dog…and walk, and walk, and walk. He is one of those dogs that doesn't like to "go". (As you become experienced as a sitter, you're finding out that there are quite a few of this type of dog.) Everything distracts him—other animals, people, a leaf blowing 100 yards away. Time is ticking on, and you have 3 other dogs to walk yet. Did I mention it's 95 degrees outside?

R.ROTH

SUZANNE M. ROTH

CHAPTER 19

The Nosy Dog

You get to the next dog. He is the one that likes to smell every blade of grass, and likes to "go" on every one of them along with every tree and bush. Time is still ticking on, and it's even hotter now. You go home and tell your husband about the incidents in CHAPTERs 18 & 19, "begging" for some comfort. He reminds you that "you could be in an office with heat in the winter and air conditioning in the summer". You're not getting any sympathy from him!!

CHAPTER 20

Driving Miss…Ally

You get a call from a pet owner who loves to walk. He walks his dog miles each morning and night. It's good exercise for both of them. You can understand that. When you go to meet them, you are asked to walk the dog for 20 minutes or so, "because he walks her at least that long, and the dog is not accustomed to going right away". Politely, you remind the customer that his dog is not the only dog you have to walk, and if you walk every dog for 20 minutes or more you will be dead from exhaustion. He tells you "but the dog must go or she will go in the house before he gets home from work". He then asks you if you would mind driving the dog—in *YOUR* car—to a "special place" where she will surely "go". You don't want to lose the customer, so you agree to take the dog in your car. Do you charge extra money for the extra time and gas, and for having to clean out your car more often? Of course not—you don't want to lose the customer. Do you get *offered* more money? Don't count on it. Wait until your husband hears this one, especially since you didn't ask for more money…and since he cleans the car…!!!

CHAPTER 21

Possessed

You have a customer for about seven years. They have two cats. One is skittish, but comes around after a while—the other is not friendly. You get a call to take care of them for two weeks. You are told that the one that isn't friendly needs a shot once a day for illness. (It's a good thing it's not the other cat that needs the shot—you'd never catch him.) The shot must be given under the skin…in his neck. You've given shots before, but aren't sure you can give them to this cat. You visit ahead of time. Your customer puts a treat in front of the cat, the cat eats the treat, and he gives him the shot assuring you that he doesn't feel it. Nothing to it. You agree to do it. Everything is fine for the first four days. You just notice that the cat is eating his treat a little faster each day. Then, you give him two treats—and he starts swallowing them whole. Then, all of a sudden, he doesn't want the treat. You are behind him. You put the treats in front of him. He starts growling at you…his body is facing the treats, and he's watching you with his head turned around. You're sure the cat is possessed, and you're thinking maybe you should call an exorcist at this point. There is no way this cat is going to let you give him this shot. You call the vet—the shot must be given in the neck. You go out and buy every different cat treat in the store. When there's one he likes, he swallows it whole, so you need to be fast—real fast! These were the slowest two weeks of your life. One good thing came out of all this—you know you have more guts than you ever thought you had!

SUZANNE M. ROTH

CHAPTER 22

Friendly? Not!

You are taking care of a Russian Blue. You are told that he had been a stray, and he's not friendly. You tell yourself, this is okay, you'll just go in, do what you need to do, and leave the cat alone. Your husband says he'll take care of this one for you. You remind him that the cat isn't friendly. While your husband is putting the cat's food down, the cat darts in. He starts rolling around your husband's feet. Your husband takes this as a friendly gesture…the cat bites his ankle. He needs a tetanus shot. The cat is now known as the "monster cat", and your husband tells you he'll never take care of the cat again, so don't even bother to ask. You remind him that just because he wants a cat to be friendly doesn't mean it will be.

CHAPTER 23

An Avoided Catastrophe

You get called to watch a German Shepherd. You go to meet him. The owner keeps insisting he's friendly (to woman only), but the dog doesn't come around you with his tail wagging like friendly dogs do. You also know that German Shepherds are very protective of their owners. This dog does not seem friendly. He lays in between you and her. Another bad feeling comes over you. You are there for almost an hour, hoping that he'll warm up to you (you keep thinking that you're not getting paid for this visit). Not once does the dog approach you. You told the lady you would do it, and she already has airline tickets. You can't tell her you can't do it now! It wouldn't be right. You go home, already worrying that you will get bit. You have two weeks before you start this dog, and he is already adding to your menage of gray hairs. You can't sleep. This doesn't feel right. How can this lady expect you to do this? Meanwhile, your husband reminds you that he can't go in for you, because the dog doesn't like men in the first place. And what if, for some reason, you can't get there—you are human, and you get sick once in a while—you can't expect him to go in! After much thought and several sleepless nights, and imagining the sleep you will lose the night before your first visit, you decide it's just not worth it. You call her. You just know that this is going to ruin your reputation. She understands, and actually seems relieved! Obviously she was a little worried, too! And perhaps she thought you were crazy all along for agreeing to do it in the first place!

CHAPTER 24

Clenched Butt Cheeks

You are called to take care of a large mixed-breed. Your husband comes with you to sign up the customer, and to meet the dog. You park the car in front of the house. The customer comes to the door, and lets the dog run out of the house. He's barking as he runs toward both of you. Your husband is ahead of you, and he's convinced this is it—this is going to be his first dog bite. Seeing a large dog running toward you is a bit intimidating. With his fingers crossed, your husband yells "what's his name?", so he can call the dog by his name. Quick thinking on his part—if a dog realizes you know his name it may stop him from biting you. It worked. The dog calmed down. (Your husband tells you later that he clenched his butt cheeks when that dog was running toward him. You tell him you were right behind him, and that you noticed.) You are both still a little concerned, because the dog seems feisty. Your first visit is a night visit. The pet owners did not leave any lights on inside the house. Of course, you bring your husband with you this time, too. The dog is barking like crazy inside. You're both convinced that this is it—one of you is going to be hurting in a minute. Both talking to the dog from outside the door and as you go in, the dog calms down. Luckily, neither of you get bit, but you get more gray hairs, and your husband attributes his first gray hair to the day he met this dog!

CHAPTER 25

The Hot House

One of the 2 cats you are taking care of needs shots. You are told that the owner has no problem getting the cat to give him his shots. You get there the first day. The cat is under the bed. He is smart enough to know not to come out. You get a broom to try to push him out. The broom isn't long enough. He runs about a foot, and he runs to a different spot under the bed. You are on the 2nd floor, and this owner happens to have their air conditioning turned off…because "cats like it hot". It is a very hot day in the middle of August. You begin to sweat. Your nerves aren't helping. You are thinking the worst—what if you can't catch him to give him the shot? What will happen to the cat? Time is ticking on again. The cat tries something new. He starts running from beneath the bed to beneath a chair. Back and forth. As he runs out, you are trying to "sweep" him into the bathroom. The bristles from the broom are falling out all over the place. You are sweating profusely. Finally, the cat runs to the bathroom! You close the door, and are able to give him the shot. This becomes a ritual for the next 7 days…causing several more gray hairs. (Why can't you just leave the cat in the bathroom? Because there are 2 cats and only one litter box. You can't leave both cats in a small bathroom—not a good idea, especially when you were not instructed to do so. What if they don't get along that well?! Most cats like their own space.

CHAPTER 26

A Devilish "Tail"

You're asked to take care of a Siamese cat. You go meet the owner and the cat. The cat is nowhere to be seen. You are told to "let him come to you", and "just don't try to pick him up". That's okay, you'll just let him warm up to you, and you won't try to pick him up. You go into the house for your first visit. The litter is down in the basement. The cat is still nowhere to be seen. After scooping the litter, you turn around to go back upstairs. The cat is at the top of the steps—he is growling at you—yes, this is not a misprint, it *is* a *cat*, and he is *growling*. He almost sounds as if he's singing. You are honest with yourself—you never knew a cat could growl. You are a little nervous. He looks as if he's ready to pounce right on you. You begin thinking of that horror movie that involves flesh-eating cats. (You knew when you were watching that movie, that you shouldn't, but you did anyway!) You think back to when your mother said "aren't you afraid of all those unfamiliar pets?", and start thinking that maybe you should be. Okay, this is silly—you realize you don't want to be down in their basement all day, and you must go past the cat to get back upstairs. He continues to sing in mad-cat language. You start clapping your hands as loud as you can (normal cats would run like the dickens)—this cat doesn't budge. There is no water in the basement to try to scare him with. You're convinced that even if there was, this cat is probably not afraid of water. You can feel the gray hairs coming in. There is a yardstick right there near his litter. You wonder why it is there…perhaps the owners knew you might need it, but didn't

-ROTH

mention it for fear that you might refuse to take care of the cat. They wanted to get away! After all, any normal person would refuse to take care of this cat, knowing this. (Thinking about it, *would* you have refused? After all, you need the money.) Of course, you would never hit the cat with the stick, but you start banging it on the stairs. It works! You decide to take it upstairs with you, just in case he's lurking around the corner. He is! You leave the yardstick at the front door for the next day. You feel better now, knowing you will be armed the next day…

SUZANNE M. ROTH

CHAPTER 27

Preventive Medicine

You are called to take care of a very old cat. She has heart problems, and must be given oral medications. You go to meet her and her owner, and are shown how you must administer the meds. The cat has her front claws. The owner does it, and it looks fairly easy. "She's used to it, and waits for the pills . You go for the first visit. There are 3 pills to be given, twice a day, as well as an aspirin every 3rd day. You pick the cat up, put her on the table, and give her the first pill—you can tell she has already had enough. She squirms, and wants to get away…already! She may be used to her owner giving her the pills—but it's going to take her longer than a week to get accustomed to you. You try talking to her, trying to keep her still. Did I mention she still has her claws? Time is ticking on. Finally, you have a brainstorm! You get your pillowcase from your bag that you keep in the car to put the cat in; this way she can't scratch you. It works, but you should have done it sooner. You've already received several "battle scars", and even worse, several more gray hairs!

CHAPTER 28

The Chariot Race

You are called to take care of two black Labrador Retrievers. You are told that they are always walked together. You know that you're not a weakling, but you also know that these two dogs are very strong. You convince yourself that you won't have a problem. Everything is going well…until one night. The dogs see a man walking a dog, and start to pull. You are not strong enough to hold them both back. They are running now, and you know that no matter what happens, you can't let those leashes go. So, you are running, too—faster than you've ever ran before. The man with the dog, a miniature poodle, keeps walking toward you. (You'd think he'd realize that he should go the other way!) The dogs (and you) are now in full stride. You feel like you're in a chariot race. When he gets close enough, he asks "what do they want?". He is completely oblivious to the fact that the dogs are acting this way, because of his dog! What does he think they want??!! You know now to wear your jogging shoes when "walking" these dogs in the future—or have your husband build a chariot!

CHAPTER 29

The Shark

The dog mentioned in CHAPTER 24 becomes a regular customer. You go there one day, and you notice he is licking his paw—it's very red and irritated. Before taking him outside, you tell him to sit, and give you his paw. He does so automatically, because you have a treat in your hand. He then realizes why you want his paw—some dogs really hate it when you try to touch the pads underneath their paws—he is one of them. He goes crazy, grabbing the sleeve of your coat. All you see are teeth. His ears are back. Suddenly, you feel like a helpless fish in a shark's mouth! He's shaking his head back and forth. You tell him "no", and luckily, he backs off. You are lucky you have your coat on! You are thinking that you won't be asking him for his paw again anytime soon, and are glad that you're not the one that cuts his nails!

CHAPTER 30

The Face of Fear

You are on your way to several different houses. You're husband is with you again. He's driving, using his own keys. All of a sudden, you tell him to "stop the car"! You don't see your key ring. You know you took it with you, but you don't *see* it. In those 1 or 2 seconds that those keys weren't in your view, indescribable panic goes through your body. Of course, the keys are right there in the car—where did you think they were??

CHAPTER 31

Retrieving a Retriever

You are walking a very large Yellow Lab. He is just about 10 months old, and doesn't listen too well yet. He walks very fast (all dogs love exercise, but Yellow Labs have *so* much energy), and pulls when you walk him. You notice he has a very thin collar for his size. You make a mental note to tell his owner. Before you get the chance, his collar snaps! Since he loves to run, as soon as he knew he was "free", off he went! Needless to say, those jogging sneakers would come in handy right about now (actually, roller skates would have been even better). He's running full speed ahead, and you are running faster than you ever thought you could. Luckily (and with God's help again, you're sure), you catch him! You leave a note for your customer, telling her what happened, and asking her to please get him a stronger collar!

CHAPTER 32

"Don't It Make Your…Blue Hair Brown"

You are taking care of a beautiful Belgian Sheepdog. His name is Bluebeard—they call him "Blue". They named him by the color of his fur—a bluish black. You don't need to walk him—there is a fenced yard. After checking the gate, you let him out. You're inside, getting his food ready. Meanwhile, the neighbor next door decides to let their dog out. They begin to run together along the fence. They probably do this all the time, but you have no idea. It wouldn't be much of a problem, if it didn't rain the night before—it's really muddy where they run. By the time you even realize what is happening (which only took about a minute), Blue is completely… brown. You can't let him back in like that! You need to wash him. Luckily, it's summer and you can wash him outside. But then, you can't let him in soaking wet, so you need to dry him. Of course, all this extra work turns into double the time. You decide not to ask for extra money. You do tell your customer what happened though, so they know you are considerate and really care about the dog, and their house. They thank you for "going above and beyond the call of duty", and you are certain you'll be called again. If this should happen again though, you will charge for an extended visit.

CHAPTER 33

Blame Where Blame Isn't Due

You are taking care of 10 cats for a week—yes, that's 10 cats (the most you've ever taken care of in one house). Sure it will be work—a lot of feeding, scooping, and cleaning up. They are all kept in the basement. You are told that 1 of them has been going out, and will really cry to go out. They don't want him out while they are away. A family member, who lives nearby, will also be coming to check on the cats. You are doing everything for them, but she is checking on them. (You know that she is probably checking on *you*, but that's okay. This is the first time you're taking care of these cats, and you can understand that people are nervous about a stranger being in the house.) After the 2nd day, the cat that usually wants to go out, was meowing like crazy—he wanted out. Of course, you tell him to forget it (as if he understands you!). The next day, you are preparing the 10 plates of food…there is silence…no meowing. The cat that has been wanting to go out is nowhere to be found. You know *you* didn't let him out. You call the family member. She tells you "she couldn't stand the cat meowing like that, so she let him out". Since no one knows exactly when he'll come back, and when he does there is a good chance neither of you will be there…you *politely* tell her this was not a good idea. You look around the neighborhood, knowing full well that even if you see the cat, you won't be able to catch him. Now what? Common sense will tell you that if you put food and water outside, the cat's belly will be full, and he'll just take off again. But then on the second day, the cat is nowhere to be seen. You start putting food outside. It is being eaten, but you don't know if *he* is eating it or a stray is eating it. The customer returns home from their trip. You make sure the first thing you tell them is that you didn't let the cat out. You are certain that the family member told a different story, because you are never called again to take care of the cats. You know in your heart that you did your job, and did everything as you were told…but who do you think they believed?

CHAPTER 34

Digging for…Well, It wasn't Gold!

A German Shepherd's owners are on vacation. You are instructed to give him a rawhide chewy after his walk. You do. During 1 visit, he comes to you. He's circling you—you know something is wrong. He starts gasping for air. You say a prayer for strength, and open his mouth. You can actually see the piece in the back of his throat. You stick your finger down his throat, scooping the piece out. It is a rather large piece. Some dogs (especially large breeds and some that are very hyperactive) don't realize that they need to *chew* rawhides into small pieces before they swallow! You will not be giving this dog any more rawhides—he'll have to wait until his owner gets home to get his rawhide! This could have been disastrous. What if you couldn't dislodge it? And what if you had already left?

CHAPTER 35

Is Someone There?

You are taking care of 2 pets in a town house. Everything is going well, until one night you get there, and there are lights on. You were there for 2 nights before this one and the lights weren't on, so you know that the lights are not on timers. You assume that the customer returned early, and just didn't call you (this happens). You look around for their car—you don't see it. There is no alarm in the house. Your imagination gets the best of you...you start thinking crazy things... like robbery...and like someone could still be in the house. You check the locks—only the knob is locked. You always lock the deadbolt when you leave after your a.m. visit. Someone has been in there—they probably got in through an unlocked window...and could still be inside! You get back in your car, and call your husband. The customer is 10 miles away, so aside from the fact that you are waiting 15 minutes for him to arrive, you are thinking about the fact that with both of you putting 20 miles each on your car and truck for this visit, you will have made exactly no money. He goes in first. Your first impulse is to ask "Is anyone there?" And then you pray no one answers! Thankfully, no one is there, and everything seems to be in place. You call the customer to ask if anyone else is supposed to have been in the house. Their response is "Oh, yes, we forgot to tell you...we are selling and the Realtor was probably by"!!!

CHAPTER 36

Adventures of a Retired Greyhound

Let the Races Begin!

You're hired to walk a Greyhound. He formerly raced, and was adopted at the age of 4. You walk him on a daily basis. As most Greyhounds are, he is very skittish. This is probably because most of the dogs used for racing haven't had much experience being treated like a pet or being loved. The first day you get there, it takes quite a few trips around the dining room table and up and down the stairs to get close to him and get his leash on. You walk him to the door, and he darts past you and out the storm door before you know it! When the door opens, he still thinks he's at the starting gate! He almost pulls your arm out of the socket; luckily, you have a tight grasp on the leash! A Greyhound, who was formerly in races is not a dog you want to have to chase—put it this way, could you catch a rabbit?

No Umbrella for This Greyhound

If it's just drizzling, you normally don't use an umbrella. On this one day, it's raining cats and…well, it's really pouring. You just washed your hair, and it's a cool day. You don't want to get sick, so you decide it's an umbrella kind of day. The dog goes out first. You lock the door behind you, and proceed to open your umbrella. The dog flips out, and starts bucking like a noosed, wild pony! He is swinging his body every which way, pulling as hard as he can to try and free himself from the leash. You are holding onto him for dear life. He is swinging back and forth—you are hoping he'll calm down, but are afraid his delicate neck is going to snap. You finally just throw the umbrella, and take the dog the other way. He may be retired, but he sure has plenty of energy!

It doesn't take long to learn what to do and what not to do. As time goes on, he warms up to you. Greyhounds are such sweet, gentle dogs. When you look into his big brown eyes, you can see how vulnerable he is. Anyway, you must always keep a tight reign on that leash! You never know when someone or something is going to scare them. (Hint: Leave the umbrella in the car!)

(Luckily, the dog wasn't hurt in any way during either incident, so you have funny stories to tell the owners—they could have been disastrous ones!)

CHAPTER 37

Cowboys and Indians

You are taking care of 2 very large collies. They are a bit on the wild side. There is no fence. There is a stake in the ground with a long line attached for each of them. The first night you take care of them, you're out with them. They are both around you, and you're petting them. All of a sudden, the neighbor 2 doors down puts their dog out on his line. The 2 collies start barking…and running. Your legs are caught in between their lines. They are running in circles, and the lines are twisting around you. Before you know it, you're in the middle of a game of cowboys and Indians. Ah, childhood memories…

CHAPTER 38

Can You Be *Too* Security Conscious?

You're taking care of 2 cats for the last time. Your customer has sold her home, and will be moving shortly. She leaves you a note, asking you to leave your key under the front mat. You take care of these cats every 2 days…which means she won't be home for 2 days. You don't like the idea of leaving her key outside for 2 days. You decide it will be better to leave it in the garage, and go out the garage door. You feel better, knowing no one can get in or make a copy of the key and put it back. Two days later, at 9:00 at night, the phone rings…your customer was going to use that key to get in! What's worse is she doesn't have the garage door opener—it's in the car inside the garage. Of course, you offer to pay for the locksmith. Most of the time, people thank you for being so conscientious. You begin to wonder if there is such a thing as being *too* security conscious!

I know you're wondering by this time if anyone needs care for pets other than cats and dogs. Don't worry, being a pet sitter you're never bored…

CHAPTER 39

All Mommies Protect Their Babies

You get a call to take care of chickens. You are sure someone is playing a joke on you, since one time you found a message on your tape asking if you also take care of zebras…! Even though the house is out of your area, you agree to do it. You go to meet the owner, and the chickens. There are 6 of them (the mother and her babies)…and 2 cats, who try to get in the pen to eat the chickens. (You wonder why someone would have chickens *AND* cats…) You are told what you need to do. The little chicks are so cute, and you ask yourself what could possibly go wrong—as long as you keep the cats out of the pen! As you write your instructions, you're telling yourself they are only chickens—they aren't really pets. Then the woman proceeds to show you pictures -many pictures— of the chickens sitting on her sofa, on her furniture, etc. They *ARE* her pets! You go for your first visit. You take your husband, because this is the only way you have time to be together. Plus, you want him to take care of the cats, and keep them out. You enter the pen -you make sure the chickens stay in, and he makes sure the cats stay out. You begin to fill the bowls. All of a sudden, the mother chicken decides to protect her babies. She begins jumping at you, making the sounds only an angry mother chicken could make, trying to peck at your face. Your husband is laughing hysterically, saying "watch your eyes!" and "God, I wish I had a video camera!". This is another story he seems to enjoy telling!

CHAPTER 40

The Miniature Dinosaur

You are called to take care of an iguana. You are told he is rather large (about 2-1/2 feet including tail). No problem, you've taken care of iguanas before. You give them your rate, based on previous iguana care. You arrange to meet the little guy and his owner. The customer calls you back the day you are to meet him to tell you there's one thing he forgot to mention—the iguana is not caged, and he has a bedroom all to himself! Okay, this is different, but you can handle it. Nothing surprises you anymore. You go to the house. A cat greets you at the door. (They forgot to mention the cat. You decide that you won't charge extra for the cat.) They take you to the bedroom, telling you the important thing is to keep the iguana *in* the room, and the cat *out*—they don't like each other very much. There are pictures of the cat both on the inside and the outside of the bedroom door…with "X's" on them to remind you to keep the cat out! You are taken into the bedroom. The iguana is up on a book shelf at eye level, which makes him look huge. He looks like a miniature dinosaur. The shelf is at your eye level. You begin to think of your mother again—how she can't believe you're not afraid of the animals…and that maybe you should be! You are told that he moves very slow, and is a gentle creature. His food and water are up on the shelf, as well. You are told that sometimes he doesn't drink, and are asked to spray bottled water into his mouth. You are asked to cut up vegetables and fruit for him each day. (You don't even cut up vegetables and fruit for yourself! He eats a more nutritious diet than you do!) You'll do it—after all, you could have been asked to feed him live crickets! You are told he is *ALWAYS* on the bottom bookshelf or on the fake plant near the shelves. You are told that it probably won't happen, but "if by chance you must pick him up, a pair of gloves will be left for you". You tell yourself that with your luck, it probably will happen, reassuring yourself that it won't. The first day everything goes well. On the second day, he is not on the shelf he's supposed to be on—he's on a smaller, higher shelf. Only *he* fits on it—his food won't fit. Well, he got up there, so he should be able to get down, right? Then you notice he didn't eat any food, which is on the lower shelf. You hold the food dish in front of him, and he eats. You spray the water into his mouth. The next day, he's still up there-his food hasn't been touched again. You are convinced that he can't get down from the shelf. He has to be able to get down to relieve himself at which time he must be able to crawl down the plant and onto the floor. The only thing to do is...put the gloves on, pick him up, and put him on the lower shelf. You muster up the nerve to pick him up—he's more afraid than you are, hanging onto you for dear life. Did I mention that his nails feel sharper than a cats? He won't let go! (More gray hairs). You keep telling yourself that iguanas are gentle creatures and they won't bite, but you keep hearing your mother saying you should be afraid. Even if he doesn't bite, he's still a tiny bit intimidating. Finally, with a little coaxing, he lets go. By the way, he moves a lot faster than they said he does. You must not forget that the cat will be waiting right outside the door, and you must be sure he doesn't get in. You check and re-check that bedroom door several times to be sure it is closed. Yet, when you leave the house you are still worrying that the cat is going to somehow get into that room!

CHAPTER 41

The Floating Fish

You are asked to take care of two tanks of fish and a turtle. Not a problem—what could possibly happen, as long as you don't over-feed the fish (in which case they can explode), and the filter doesn't malfunction. You do everything you're supposed to do—yet you still find a floating fish. What do you do? Do you flush it down the toilet or throw it in the trash? With your luck it probably has a name, they've had him a long time, and he's probably the little boy's favorite fish! If this is the case, he will probably want to give it a proper burial when he gets back. You don't want it to get smelly or worse, like become the cat's dinner—so you wrap it in plastic wrap and put it in the freezer. You're just glad you don't have to be the one to explain all of this to the little boy. When the owners get home, you extend your sympathies. They reassure you that it wasn't your fault, and that fish die all the time. You know from this experience to ask future fish owners what to do in case of death.

CHAPTER 42

To Catch a Cockatoo

You are asked to take care of birds—a Cockatoo and 2 Parakeets. Normally, all you need to do with birds is feed them and change their cage once or twice during the week. You quote a rate based on jobs that you've done in the past. (You haven't learned yet.) You go to meet them, and you are told that they want you to take the birds out of the cages for exercise. The cockatoo likes to play dead in your lap, and be pet under her wings. Then she plays on her gym. Then you put her in her cage, and take the other birds out. You can't take them all out at the same time, because the Cockatoo can hurt the parakeets. "They all go back in with no problem...as long as they're out long enough". Of course, the birds' opinion of long enough is different than yours. Needless to say the cockatoo doesn't feel she's had enough play time, and refuses to go back in her cage . She starts playing "catch me if you can". When you do catch her she hooks her beak onto the cage, refusing to get off your hand. You find yourself talking to yourself, and telling her she's a bad bird. You finally get her in, and then you have the parakeets to contend with. You have a problem the first day—they don't want to go back in the cages either. On the 2nd day you learn a trick—they love millet sprays, so you hang a couple inside the cage. They go in with no problem! You have outsmarted the parakeets! The bottom of the Cockatoo's cage must be scrubbed, her gym wiped off, and you must also change the papers in the cages every day. Needless to say, all of this is taking much longer than a normal visit (actually, you begin wondering what a "nor-

THE REALITY OF PROFESSIONAL PET SITTING   71

-ROTH

mal" visit is anymore.) You decide that you will be increasing your fee the next time you are called for these birds…but you don't want to lose the customer. Maybe, you won't. Oh, did I mention that you are asked to come after 4:00, because that's when the mail comes? This throws your whole schedule off. You usually like to be home between 4 and 6:00, so you can have dinner with your husband, and get ready to go back out again at 7:00 or so. So much for scheduling your time!

CHAPTER 43

The World's Largest Green House

You are asked if you would mind watering plants, since you'll be there taking care of a couple of pets. You mention to the new customer that watering plants is included in your services. The customer is ecstatic that you offer this service. When you're asked if there will be an additional charge, you say "No". You can still picture the look on your face when you walked to the back of the house, and saw the largest greenhouse ever built! (Will you *ever* learn?! You're beginning to wonder!)

IS PROFESSIONAL PET SITTING FOR YOU?

DO YOU HAVE A RELIABLE CAR? That's all you'll need, *if* you live in a part of the country that's warm all the time. If you live in a state where it snows, you will need a reliable 4-wheel drive truck. People go away to warm places in the winter (you can't blame them). It is your job to worry about how you're going to get to their house in a storm. It is your job to get there. Then, once you get there, you'll need to be able to get in driveways. And, of course, the wind is always blowing towards the door that you have to go in, leaving snowdrifts blocking it. Ice storms are even more fun. No car or truck handles well on ice. (Case in point, see CHAPTER 2.) (I often wonder if there are pet sitters in Alaska—I must make a note to contact them, and find out how they get around in ice storms! Even though I don't like the idea of dogs pulling sleds, that's probably the only way!)

The next logical question would be "DO YOU LIKE TO DRIVE"? You had better LOVE to drive. If you really want to get into business, you will take any customer, no matter where you need to go. Of course, your first two customers will live 20 minutes away from each other, and even after you are established and have more customers closer together, you will still be spending more time on the road than actually pet sitting.

Perhaps the *MOST* logical question is "DO YOU LIKE TO WALK"? When you are a pet sitter, you walk, and walk, and walk. You need a lot of energy. As luck would have it, most people that live in apartment buildings live on the 2nd or 3rd floor; and with all the new townhouses around, many customers live in the furthest one from the parking lot. Then, you must walk each dog at least 10 to 15 minutes (longer if the dogs are like the ones mentioned in CHAPTERs 18 and 19). Let's figure on 15 minutes per dog, and 7 visits per day, as an average. 7 visits a day times 15 minutes per dog—you will be walking 1-3/4 to 2 hours per day on an average day just for the dogs, and not including walking to and from your car. (In the summer and once you get established, you may have 10 to 12 visits per day including dogs, cats, etc., which means you will be walking an average of 3 hours per day.)

ARE YOU SELF-MOTIVATED? Since you will be working for yourself, there will be no one telling you what to do. *You* are responsible for generating business. *You* are responsible for taking care of business. *You* are responsible for your own success.

ARE YOU A RELIABLE AND DEPENDABLE PERSON? It's raining, snowing, sleeting or you are feeling sick. Will you be willing to get out there—driving to all those houses, shoveling those entryways that may need to be shoveled, and walking the dogs that need to be walked? (Case in point, see CHAPTERs 1 & 2.) On a gorgeous summer day, will you be willing to give up a day at the beach to take care of the pets you have scheduled?

ARE YOU A "MORNING" PERSON? You may have 3 dogs to walk—you can't get to any of them later than 8:30 or you will no doubt find some big messes to clean up in the houses. Depending on how far you need to drive to get to each of them (we'll say 15 minutes), and considering you must spend 25 minutes with each of them (unless for some reason you need to extend your visit)—you will need to be out of the house by 6:00 a.m.

DO YOU LIKE TO RELAX? (Perhaps a better question would be "ARE YOU A STRONG PERSON {MENTALLY})?" With a "normal" job, you get home at a certain time, and you are done. A pet sitter must go out in the morning and night (sometimes in the afternoon, as well) for "vacation" dogs, and in the afternoon to walk the dogs for the owners who are at work, as well as for the cats, lizards, fish, turtles, rabbits and birds. A sitter then must to out at 7:30-8:00 at night to walk dogs, getting home at 9:30-10:00 or so, depending on the number of dogs needing care. At times you will be asked to visit at 10:00 p.m., because that's when the dog is usually walked for the last time in the evening. As luck would have it, usually you will have this dog to walk when you have no others. Your body is telling you to relax, but you can't because you have to go out at 9:30 p.m. This is particularly fun in the winter months. Then, there are the phone calls you need to return, and the customers you need to sign up (usually at night, since most people aren't home during the day).

ARE YOU A STRONG PERSON (PHYSICALLY)? (Case in point, see CHAPTERs 11 & 12.) With any luck, this sort of thing doesn't happen often—but you must be able to pick up a dog should the need arise. Also, most cat owners buy the largest bags of litter, understandably, to save money—these bags are pretty heavy. (You may be scooping every day, but as a courtesy you still need to change the litter before your customer returns home. (And just wait until you see where those litter boxes are stashed!) Plus, you'll need a strong back and strong legs to get in and out of your car or truck on an average of 14 times per day based on 7 visits.

ARE YOU CONSTANTLY CONCERNED ABOUT YOUR AP-PEARANCE? If so, start learning to juggle. Say it's raining. You're trying to hold up an umbrella (this is especially fun when it's also windy!), while holding a leash (or two) and the dog(s) are pulling, while getting a plastic bag out of your pocket, while taking your gloves off, while bending over to pick up poohs, while trying to keep your scarf from falling into the poohs. Since you only have two hands, after once or twice, you realize something's got to go.

Since you can't let go of the dog(s), the only other option is the umbrella. (For a perfect example, see CHAPTER 36.) The worst part is, it's been raining a lot lately!

DO YOU HAVE SELF-ESTEEM? I know you're wondering why on earth you will need self-esteem for this job. Think about it. You'll certainly need it when you're walking around soaking wet. You'll need it while you are talking to a potential customer on the phone, and when you go to meet them. You don't have a product to sell...basically, you are selling yourself. You will be meeting a lot of people. *They don't come to you, you must go to them.* You will need it when people ask you what you do for a living, and you tell them you are a pet sitter. The usual response is "you're a what?!!?". Try telling people, especially those who don't have any pets or hate animals (hard to imagine, but they do exist), that you pick up poohs, clean throw ups and litter boxes, feed chickens and clean their pens, feed iguanas that aren't in cages, and take care of pigs for a living. The most common responses are "not for all the money in the world" and "you're nuts".

DO YOU HAVE PATIENCE? You will need this (even if you answered "yes" to the last question) when people joke about what you have to do to make a living (and they will). They'll say they're "just joking", but they still assume that you're too dumb to do anything else. After all, if you have other skills, why on earth would you rather pick up dog poohs and scoop cat litter? YOU'LL NEED PATIENCE when you find "pet mistakes" in the houses from time to time that you will need to clean up. YOU'LL NEED PA-TIENCE when you're walking a dog that stops to smell everything in his path. YOU'LL NEED PATIENCE when you're walking a dog that stops whenever he sees something—anything—moving within 1000 feet. (Imagine the fun when it's a blustery day in November, and there are a million leaves blowing—this type of dog notices each and every one of them, and will not pooh until everything is still (plan on a prolonged visit when you are walking this type of dog on a windy day!). (See CHAPTERs 18 and 19.) YOU'LL NEED PATIENCE when you get a call from a potential customer, and you're told that your price is too high. You are then called back—they've changed their mind (probably because they can't get anyone to do it for less or for free). You need the money, so you take the job. Did I mention that they are leaving the next day, so you have no choice but to go over to their house that day. Oh, did I mention that your parents are visiting, so you have no choice but to leave them in your house while you go sign the customer up? You tell them that you'll be right back…which turns out to be a fib…they have 8 cats, which turns into a lot of instructions. You can't rush through a pre-sitting visit for any reason. You are there for an hour, talking and writing instructions. Then, someone calls. You're sitting there, and you have a bad feeling. When they finally get off the phone, you are told "we're not sure yet". (Did I mention they're supposedly leaving the next day? You begin to wonder when they will be sure.) No doubt, the person on the phone said they would take care of the cats. Perhaps this person is not reliable…but they're cheaper. You've already wasted over an hour of your time, while your parents are waiting for you back at your house. By this time, you're not very happy. You tell them (politely and patiently, of course…) that you will not be back. YOU'LL NEED PATIENCE when you tell a potential customer your rate, and they laugh at you and tell you they'll get a neighborhood kid to do it for a buck. YOU'LL NEED PATIENCE when 1 out of every 3 calls you get is from a person that wants to be a pet sitter. (Everyone thinks it's such an easy job-after all, how hard could it be to walk dogs and feed cats? Plus, there's probably no overhead, right?) Of course, when they call they don't tell you they're calling because they want to be your competitor and take food off of your table—they pretend to be potential customers. You may have a gut feeling that you are speaking with a potential sitter, but you can't be sure (a crystal ball would come in handy in this situation!). So, you proceed to tell them all about your services…and then find them listed in the newspaper as a pet sitter a few days later! (Your first clue should have been when they told you that they "envy" you. The second clue should be when they ask what you base your rates on (if they have 1 dog, why would they care what you charge for 3?). The first consolation is that they have a rude awakening coming—because pet sitting is not as easy as everyone seems to think it is. The second consolation is that contrary to what people think, pet sitters do have overhead. Foremost is the gas—not to mention the mileage that you will be putting on your car. Then there's advertising. You'll need to create effective flyers and business cards. Then there are printing charges for them, as well as contracts and brochures. Ads in newspapers are also costly. It is also time-consuming to walk your flyers around. You can hire someone, but be sure it's someone you know and trust. The flyers need to be delivered—not end up in the garbage. If you want to be a professional, you should also get yourself bonded, and consider purchasing insurance.) YOU'LL NEED PATIENCE when, just as your time and effort begins to pay off, another sitter comes along and starts tearing down all your flyers and plastering hers all over the place. Everywhere you go, her flyers are up, and yours are down. You begin to swear, and swear you are being stalked. Luckily, nightmares such as this don't happen to all pet sitters—it's just happening to you, because you're so lucky. This person is from out of state, and yet out of all the states in the country, and all the cities in your state, she had to pick yours to start an unprofessional business. You don't mind competition, but this is ridiculous. She doesn't want to be your competitor—she wants you out of business. Period. It truly is a "dog eat dog world" -no pun intended. After a year or so, you find she has moved out of your area, and you thank God, again. YOU'LL NEED PATIENCE when you commit yourself to walk a dog 3 days a week. It's summertime. You walk the dog about 2:00 in the blistering sun, as instructed, for several weeks. The customer tells you how happy he is, and how happy the dog is when he gets home. Then, all of a sudden he calls to tell you that you are not needed for a week. You have a feeling something is up. The following week, you are told that the customer's neighbor will be walking the dog from now on—but he'll call you "if the neighbor can't do it". Well, isn't that kind of him? Of course, you can understand why your customer would rather have his neighbor walk the dog. He is surely taking less money. And you can understand why the neighbor would offer—after all, he's just being neighborly. However, the harsh reality is that you can't make a living this way. If everyone did this to you, you'd be out of business. Do you think patience will come in handy now? Believe it or not, some people honestly don't realize that this is a real job, and that you are not doing this as a hobby. YOU'LL NEED PATIENCE when you pull into a driveway, and realize you don't have that person's key on your ring. This means driving home to get it, which will make the dog and customer happy, but will put you behind on your schedule—or not going home to get it, and ruining your reputation. It's your call.

DOES YOUR HUSBAND HAVE PATIENCE? Perhaps, this is a better question to ask yourself. (Disregard this question, if you are not married, and don't ever intend to be while in the pet-sitting profession.) HE'LL NEED PATIENCE when you come home every day, furious over someone constantly taking your flyers down…obviously trying to steal all of your business. (With any luck, this won't happen to you.) HE'LL NEED PATIENCE, especially if he has his own full-time job, when he's asked to help with some visits because you have overbooked yourself. (You tend to overbook in the summer and on the weekends or on a holiday when the rest of the world is having fun with their family or away on vacation). HE'LL NEED PATIENCE when he's asked to come with you on a Saturday night, because it's the only way you can be together. HE'LL NEED PATIENCE if you get sick, and he needs to take a week's vacation to do your pets. HE'LL NEED PATIENCE when you ask him to come with you, because you will be going into a risky neighborhood and you're a little nervous. HE'LL NEED PATIENCE when he's asked to come with you when you're visiting a large dog for the first time, and you think he's going to bite (you'd like him to come so he can walk in the house first). HE'LL NEED PATIENCE when a cat bites his ankle for no reason whatsoever. HE'LL NEED PATIENCE when is asked to come with you to fix a screen on a front door (the one you had to rip to unlock the inner door). HE'LL NEED PATIENCE when there's an ice storm, and you must go out anyway—he knows you're afraid to drive on ice (who isn't?), and he'll want to go with you. HE'LL NEED PATIENCE when, after he has just shoveled his own driveway and steps, he has to come with you to shovel the steps at your customers' houses. HE'LL NEED PATIENCE when he's asked to come and pick up Mr. Squirrel, who has fallen from a tree in front of a customer's door. HE'LL NEED PATIENCE when he's asked to come with you in the middle of the night, because one of your customer's alarm is blaring, and you are on the list to be called by the alarm company. HE'LL NEED PATIENCE when he wants to go away for a day on the weekend, and you tell him it's impossible, because you have pets scheduled. HE'LL NEED PATIENCE when he says "it's been 3 years since we've had a vacation—let's go away", and you tell him you can't because you have visits scheduled for the next couple of months. (You don't want to lose any more customers like you did the last time you took a vacation.) HE'LL NEED PATIENCE when he wants to go to a movie, and you tell him you'll have to go to a matinee "in between your pet sitting visits". HE'LL NEED PATIENCE when you tell him that you took new customers, because your schedule wasn't completely full, and then a couple of customers that you've had before call for the same time and you took them too—so now you're overbooked. (After all, you didn't want to lose any of your repeat customers!) (A crystal ball would come in handy again! If you knew the old customers needed you before the new ones called, you wouldn't have taken the new ones.) Sorry to say, there's no way to avoid overbooking.

DO YOU LIKE TO SLEEP? Depending on how conscientious you are, you can lose a lot of sleep over this job. Why, you ask?

Reason Number 1

You get into bed. You're exhausted. All of a sudden, your mind starts racing…after you let the dogs back in, did you lock the back doors? Did you check all the windows on the first floor of all the houses to be sure they were locked? Did you turn all the lights on that are supposed to be on? Did you turn the lights off that are not supposed to be left on? Did you turn off the faucet after you filled Fido's dish? Did you check to be sure the toilet, the one you were told to use to flush Kitty's litter—the one that sometimes doesn't stop running—stopped running? (Of course you did all these things—after a while they become automatic…yet you *still* question yourself.)

Reason Number 2

The night before you start a job (usually while in bed trying to sleep), you'll wonder if you're going to get bit when you first walk into a house with a new dog—especially if they didn't seem that friendly. And more so if the dog is very large or is usually kenneled, and never left home with a strange person coming in. Pet owners say their dogs are friendly; they may actually believe this. The fact is, they are not going to be there, and neither of you can say how the dog is going to react. Some people know their dogs are protective, but won't tell you—after all, they want to get away and they know there aren't a whole lot of people willing to get their hands bit off for a small fee. They only know they don't want to kennel their dog, and they want to go away. (Think about when *you* want to get away; especially if you've already paid the money.) 99% of the time all the worrying is for nothing…but it still can't hurt to say a few prayers.

Reason Number 3

The night before you start a job (again, usually in bed while trying to sleep), you'll be wondering if you will be able to disarm the customer's alarm in time. (See CHAPTERs 6, 9 & 10.)

Reason Number 4

You will be caring for a dog and 5 cats. The owner says the cats are all friendly, and none of them are "hiders". The first day, you only see 4 cats. You assume you'll see the 5th tomorrow. You don't. The panic sets in. There is no way you can tell by the food or the waste in the litter box, since there are 4 other cats. You start looking everywhere they could be hiding. No cat. You're sure he's gone. Of course, he isn't—it's amazing how many places a cat can hide. You know you didn't let him out. But you still don't see him. What if he got out while you were taking the dog out? You know he didn't get past you—but then, where is he? You can stop holding your breath when you finally see him!

Reason Number 5

With thoughts of the incident in CHAPTER 4, will you see another mouse when you walk in? Worse yet, will you step on a dead one?

Reason Number 6

Your husband is taking care of 3 cats for you. They are Blue Russians. He comes home after the second day, and tells you he hasn't seen the 3rd cat. You know you can trust your husband, and he didn't let the cat out—but can you sleep? Not until he tells you he's seen that 3rd cat!

Reason Number 7

With thoughts of the incident in CHAPTER 12, imagine knowing you must go back to that house. After all, it wouldn't be right to call the owner in another state and tell him he'd better come home! This is something a Professional Pet Sitter will avoid at all costs!

Reason Number 8

You are in bed, imagining you lost the keys to all those houses! (See CHAPTER 30.) You are having a nightmare, and you haven't even slept yet!

Reason Number 9

Did you forget to write a pet on your calendar? Are you going to get a call from an irate customer, and justifiably so, because you forgot to take care of their pets for a week? Of course, this has never happened to me. I worked in an office for 20 years; I am very organized, and I know how to schedule. But, I have gotten calls from people looking for a new sitter, because of this reason. Which brings me to the next question.

DO YOU KNOW HOW TO SCHEDULE? I mean, are you a really good scheduler? You may have 12 visits to make in one day (for vacation dogs, you will be visiting 2 or 3 times each per day, plus "daily walkers", plus the cats (sometimes 2 times a day if a cat is on medication) and other small animals. In between you will need to sign up new customers. Of course, 95% of them are only home at night, so along with walking dogs at night, you will be signing up customers. And don't forget all those phone calls you need to make. You better know how to schedule your time.

ARE YOU A WORRIER? If so, do not hire other pet sitters to help you. Aside from the fact that most potential customers ask who will be coming into their home, and prefer the owner to an employee, how can you be 100% certain your employee is trustworthy? Remember, they will be going into homes they've seen only in their dreams. Also, how do you know that he/she will not decide to go to the shore instead of helping you, leaving you with *double* visits to do?

ARE YOU PREPARED TO GIVE UP YOUR HOLIDAYS AND YOUR WEEKENDS? (*If you have help*, you're lucky if you can rely on them completely at these times. Not too many employees are willing to give up their weekends and holidays, unless they are extremely reliable or are making *all* the money.)

DO YOU HAVE GOOD ORGANIZATIONAL SKILLS? Some pet owners, when they realize they can trust you, will eventually ask you to hold onto their keys. You will need to find a way to keep these keys organized, so you will know which key belongs to which customer. You will also need to keep all contracts up to date, and have a good filing system.

DO YOU HAVE A COMPUTER? My husband had asked if I wanted one. I said I didn't, and they're too much money. He got it anyway, and I can't stress enough how much I use it.

WILL YOU BE MAKING ENOUGH MONEY TO PAY ALL YOUR BILLS? If not, you'll just "fill in" with another part-time job, right? You'd just get another job in the a.m.—no, in the afternoon—no, in the p.m.—no, overnight, of course! Face the reality—you can't get another job, because you haven't gotten your hands on a crystal ball yet. Pet sitters don't know their schedule sometimes until one week ahead. Even if you only have 1 dog 3 times a day—there's no way you can commit to another job.

DO YOU LIKE TO TRAVEL? Do you like to take summer vacations? Remember that summer will be your busiest time. Depending on how serious you are about being a professional sitter, it will be a good 3 years before you'll feel free to take a vacation and not worry about losing customers.

DO YOU HAVE SMALL CHILDREN? If so, you will find it very difficult to do your job. You must be available at all times of the day to be a pet sitter.

WILL YOU MIND PICKING UP POOHS? Before you answer, you must mentally picture the scene. Cars are driving by. No one is noticing you. Then, you pick up the poohs, and all of a sudden everyone is watching! Oh, it's even better when there are construction guys or grass cutters all over the place. There you are trying to have some finesse, while trying to be inconspicuous…yeah, sure. Face it, you're picking up poohs for heaven's sake!

WILL YOU MIND HAVING DOGS PUT THEIR BEHIND IN YOUR FACE? It seems that every dog, if they like you, turns their back to you—they want their butts scratched!

SOME ADVICE

—If you are married, think long and hard before you commit yourself to pet sitting, and only if you have a VERY understanding and extremely patient husband! (One that can adapt easily to any situation-and is willing to do so!) Sit down with your husband to discuss it. Since you've read the incidents that happened to me, you know you can't just assume that he'll put up with what he may be confronted with. Talk about it! The first word you'll want to learn how to say is "no" (not to him—to your customers, of course!). Otherwise, they will have you out at all times of the day, 7 days a week (for example, some people will ask you to come at 5:00 a.m. or at 10:00 p.m. "because that's the time the dog is usually walked"). Never under any circumstances agree to an overnight stay. Your husband is putting up with enough, and you want to keep your happy marriage happy. Be warned, however, that when you do learn the "no" word, you will lose customers, especially now that there are pet sitters popping up everywhere. However, if you don't learn it, you could end up losing your family life.

—If you have small children, don't even attempt pet sitting. You need to be out in the morning, afternoon, and night. If you do become a sitter, remember that people do not want children in their houses (some pets are actually afraid of children, because they are not usually around them). Also, a pet can easily sneak by a child when all of you are entering the home or leaving. To be professional, leave your children at home. (This will require additional patience on your husband's part—or money in your budget for a baby sitter!)

—If you have pre-teen or teenage children, never send one of them in your place. The responsibility is too great for children. Some dogs are too large for them to handle. Also, they could forget to lock one of the doors. Any number of things could happen, and guess who would be blamed…

—If you are a man, it will be difficult to get established as a pet sitter. In my experience approximately 85% of pet owners needing services are women. Understandably, they trust another woman with the key to their home before they will trust a man. Also, some customers say their pets "don't like men as much"; others say they "don't like men at all" (See CHAPTERs 12 & 23). (This is probably because they are not around them as much.)

—If your hair color is natural and void of grays, and you want to keep it that way, don't become a pet sitter. If you're a "dye hard" (no pun intended) and you still want to give it a try, stock up on some boxes of hair coloring—you'll need them.

—If you need a steady and constant income, remember that there will be months that you will make a lot of money, and other months that you will make no money. There is no telling what you will make in a year. (I'm still looking for that crystal ball!) This is determined by how many customers you have, how often they travel, and how many other sitters decide to enter into pet sitting in your area. As in most businesses, you will not see a decent profit for a couple of years. Most difficult is getting your name out to the public (as I mentioned earlier in the book, most people don't even realize pet sitters exist), and even when you finally do get your name around, there will always be some people who are unwilling to trust you with their keys until you have plenty of references.

Like any job, people want "experience", which is not easy to get when you don't have references yet!

—Expect your own pets, dogs especially, to turn their nose(s) up at you. They won't be happy when they first find out that you have been in the company of other pets. How will they know? Believe me, their noses never fail. This may sound silly, but I know it is true.

—Get yourself bonded and insured, even though it takes quite a few visits to pay these bills. *After you have been in business for a few years and if you've never had to file a claim, talk with your insurance agent to decide if you need to continue your insurance. This is not an easy decision to make. Use your discretion.

—If you haven't yet, learn how to pump your own gas. You'll be using a lot of it, and it will be much cheaper.

—Only take customers that live within 10 miles of each other.

—Send News Releases to local newspapers. Be sure they get all the facts straight, and the phone number is put in correctly. Yes, this has happened to me. I was so excited that my business was going to be mentioned in the paper! Then the wrong phone number was printed. They ruined my "day in the sun". They "corrected" it by correcting the number in the "correction" part of the paper. First of all, you had to know to even look for a correction, and when you found it was so tiny, you needed a magnifying glass to see it!

—If you have never had a tetanus shot or haven't had one in the past 10 years, get one. Don't wait until you get bit or you are walking a dog through some woods and get a rusty nail in your foot.

—Trust your feelings. If you have bad vibes a about a dog, believe in your instincts! A customer won't usually tell you a dog isn't friendly, but might say the dog is "protective". I always say "the money I'm making is not worth getting my hand bit off!"

—If a customer *tells* you a cat isn't friendly, don't take it personal. If he/she gives you the appearance of being friendly, don't believe it!

—If you have a full-time job and you are really serious about getting started in pet sitting, if you want to *keep* your sanity *let go* of your other job. (The expression "something's got to give" applies here. Believe me, I know.) As you have read, sometimes what you think will be "normal" pet-sitting visits turn into longer visits, and you don't want to rush the care of a pet. Something's got to give, and you don't want it to be your reputation.

—Do not overbook, to keep your sanity. Sometimes you just can't avoid it. If you find yourself in that situation, never assume that you can just skip a cat or two for a day thinking that he/she will be fine for one day. You won't get away with it. You may not think so, but there will always be a neighbor whose assignment is to watch you. Some customers will even tell you that they have neighbors watching the house; especially, the first time they hire you. The customer could even come home early from their trip. Don't take chances. All it takes is once.

—Just because a customer is using your services, doesn't mean they will forever. People move, whether it be for their jobs or from an apartment to a house that happens to be in another county, and so on. You'll wonder why they can't just stay in one place for a while. Also, there is a big turnover for daily walkers. People may hire your services just until their puppy becomes an adult. You never know when you're going to lose a customer; it usually happens suddenly, and you're the last to know. The point I'm making is, keep your name out there. Don't stop advertising, because you feel you have enough customers at the present time.

—Even if you don't have any help, you must have a back-up—someone you can depend on during those times when you are too sick to leave the house (remember, you are human!).

—Never rely on your memory. Even if you have a terrific memory, don't count on it. When you remember that something needs to be done, do it as soon as you think of it, if you can (to avoid incidents like the one in CHAPTER 3). If you can't do it right then, write it down immediately! ALWAYS write the dates you are needed on your calendar *immediately* after talking with a customer. Just think of how you'd feel if you forgot a customer's pet for a whole week! How you'd feel is irrelevant—it wouldn't give you a good reputation!! Also, you'll be "on call" for your corporate customers. You'll get last minute calls and cancellations. Even worse than forgetting to visit a pet is visiting when you're not supposed to! Walking into someone's house when you shouldn't be there gives you a really strange feeling (especially when they're home), and can be very dangerous.

—Never walk a dog without a leash.

—If a customer wants you to leave a dog in a fenced yard while they are away, first of all try convincing them that this is not a good idea. If the gate is not locked, children that sometimes vist could forget to close it again. Even if the gate will be locked, the dog could decide to dig himself out because of loneliness, another dog, any number of reasons. If the customer insists, walk around the fence with the client to find any potential "escape routes"—any areas where the pet may already be "making his mark"—and for any loose fencing. Ask them to put a lock on the gate, if there isn't an existing one. If the dog is large, ask them if the pet has ever jumped the fence. If he has, ask them where he/she is likely to go if he/she does jump.

—Before you ever let any dog into a fenced yard, always check the gates!

—Never give a price, until you are sure of what you will be required to do. And don't ever expect anyone to *OFFER* a little extra money for the time it takes for you to do jobs "above and beyond your duty"—not too many will.

—Always ask if others will be entering the house while your customer is away. If so, why will they be entering? Ask if they will be taking the dog for a walk or taking the dog out in their car, so if the dog isn't there when you get there, you'll know why, and if there's a yard, you'll know to be certain to check the gate before you let the dog out. Will they be feeding the dog? You don't want to both be feeding him/her. (Of course, the dog wouldn't mind!) It's also good to know if someone else will be in the house in case the owners find something wrong (such as something missing {like a pet!} or whatever else). (See CHAPTER 33.) Usually it's best if no one else will be entering. Of course, you can't tell your customer whom to let in their house!

—Ask the customer if there is *anything* you should know.

—Always remind your customers to leave their storm door unlocked to avoid incidents like the one in CHAPTER 7.

—Have a supply of sturdy key rings on hand. If a customer gives you a key on a flimsy ring, change it right away or as soon as you get to your office. (See CHAPTER 3.)

—Establish an effective "key" system. A numbering system works well. When you have the keys to your customers' houses, you want to be able to find the one you need in an instant. There should be no question whether or not it is the right key. You don't want to fumble with 100 keys at your customer's house to find the right one. (You can be sure one of the neighbors will report that to your customer!)

—Purchase a safe to keep your keys in. It will give both you and your customers peace of mind. If your house is robbed, and they get their hands on all those keys…well, I think you can figure it out…you had the keys, you will probably get blamed.

—If you have a customer's key, and you haven't serviced them in a while, ask if they've changed their locks since you were there last. Also, ask if an alarm has been installed.

—Always complete a contract, and have the customer sign it.

—Think "Check—then double-check". When a customer gives you dates, check—then double-check" to be sure you've written the correct dates on your calendar; every morning, before leaving the house, "check—then double-check" your calendar so what you need to do that day is fresh in your mind; "check—then double-check" to be sure you have the keys you need for that day on your key ring (nothing's worse than pulling up to a house and realizing you don't have the key); and while on the job, always "check—then double-check" yourself to be sure you're leaving the pet(s) and the house per the owner's instructions.

—Always ask if there is an alarm in the house, and if the customer will be using it while they are away.

—Keep a spare leash in your car in case the owner forgets to tell you where their leash is kept. (Try to remember to ask this question though to avoid the type of incident noted in CHAPTER 12.)

—Purchase books on pets. When someone calls and tells you they have an "Alaskan Malamute", you don't want to need to ask if that

is a breed of dog or cat! It helps to know what the pet looks like—
if he/she is large or small, etc. Books on illnesses and how to spot
them are also helpful.

—Keep emergency supplies in your car; e.g., tweezers, and alco-
hol for ticks; a spare leash in case the owner doesn't leave one;
cotton balls and peroxide (mix 1 part peroxide to 9 parts water) in
case you need to clean a dog's ears. (Some dogs have problems
with their ears. If a dog is shaking his head constantly, this can
cause damage. You can't wait a week until the owner gets back); a
spray for hot spot relief; first aid spray; a pillowcase to put cats in
that have claws, and they need to be medicated and won't cooper-
ate; a cat carrier in case you can't find the owner's in an emergency;
a sheet to cover your car seat should you need to transport a sick
pet, and a blanket to cover the pet.

—Stock up on eye refreshers/moisturizers. Namely, the ones that
get the red out. You'll need them after those sleepless nights. Buy
stock in this company, as well!

—Stock up on your vitamins—for example, B vitamins for stress,
and Vitamin C for when you are exposed to the elements and the
germs that may be lurking in the houses you'll be entering.

—Wash your hands before leaving each house. Carry anti-bacte-
rial wipes with you in your car.

—Stock up on flea and tick repellent to spray on your clothes
during the summer months.

—If you don't have a 4-wheel drive or an all-wheel drive vehicle,
get one. You *must* be able to get where you're going even in the
nastiest weather.

—If you don't have an answering machine, get one. (This is your most important tool, since you are never home to answer the phone!)

—If you don't have a car phone, get one. What a relief in an emergency!

If you have gotten this far, and you still want to give Professional Pet Sitting a try, you must be a determined, persistent person with a strong will—two of the many vital qualities needed!

WHAT IT TAKES
TO BE SUCCESSFUL

Although it is a necessary quality, loving animals is not all it takes to be a Professional Pet Sitter. The kind of love a sitter has for animals goes way beyond the norm. I tell people who think they would like to be a pet sitter to think of their own dog (they most likely have one), and to think of all the other dog owners out there. If they are honest with themselves, they will admit that even though they love their dogs, they don't always love walking them early in the morning, sometimes walking them on their lunch hour, and walking them at night. All pet owners love their pets, but sometimes don't like the demands being a pet owner puts on them. Becoming a pet sitter means walking dogs…lots of dogs…in all kinds of weather. When a true pet lover first hears about pet sitting, especially if they are unhappy with their current job or they don't have a job, their first thought is "that sounds like something I would like to do". Through the years, I can't count how many times I've heard people say that. After all, how hard is it to take care of pets? The truth is, it is not the toughest job in the world, but it certainly isn't as easy as everyone seems to think. I've given you examples of some of the things that can go array when you are performing your duties as a pet sitter. You probably realize now that becoming a Professional Pet Sitter is not as easy as you thought, and that being successful is hard work. This is why you will see a new company advertise for a while, and then you find they are out of business. You really can get "burned out". In my years as a Professional Pet Sitter I have seen many sitters come and

SUZANNE M. ROTH

go. I am certain that every one of them started their business with a dream of becoming independent and wealthy.

In order to become a *professional* sitter, there are many attributes a person must have. In my opinion highest on the list of these attributes are dedication, reliability, trustworthiness, determination, persistence, availability—and the list doesn't stop there.

If you are self-motivated, work well independently, have the will to generate business, and the determination and dedication to put in the necessary time, you will reap the advantages of this profession. Remember, *you* are responsible for making your business a success!

THE ADVANTAGES OF PROFESSIONAL PET SITTING

—Since your business is based on animals, you will be meeting and caring for many sweet animals. Taking care of them is your primary duty. If you truly love all animals, you will be one of those lucky people who loves their job.

—You will meet some very nice people, too!

—No experience is "mandatory". You must, of course, be an "animal" person, and it helps to have pets of your own. You must also be personable, since you will be meeting a lot of people. It also helps to have some business experience behind you, which will help you organize your business.

—Technically, you are your own boss. Though in reality, you will have many bosses (namely, the pet owners).

—You can schedule personal appointments (e.g., doctor and dental visits, hair appointments) during the day instead of having to go after 5:00 p.m. or on a Saturday when everyone else in the world is there, too. (Of course, you will need to schedule them in between your sitting visits, which can be a bit unnerving when your appointment is at 11:00 and you're still waiting at 11:30.)

SUZANNE M. ROTH

—As long as you know how to say "no", and can accept the fact that you may lose a customer or two, you can take a day or a week off whenever you want to. However, keep in mind "if you don't make the visits, you don't make the money".

—Once you get established, you are free to decide which jobs you will accept, and which you don't feel you should do (this takes a while, but if you hang in there you will get to this point).

—There will be days when you have *NO* pets. (Yes, I've put this under the correct heading. Everyone needs a break every once in a while—not too often, though!). Of course, the longer you are in business, the more rare and precious these days are—and even though you will have no income on such days, you will welcome them. Trust me.

—There is no dress code. Animals don't care if you're wearing jeans. (Of course, you will want to look presentable when you go to meet a new customer.)

YOU KNOW YOU'VE MADE IT WHEN:

—You decide you are going to set a weekend aside (maybe even a whole week!) to take a vacation…and you don't cancel it when you get calls for that weekend/week! You realize that since you work just about 365 days a year, you need to get away once in a while! You know that you may lose some customers, but you have a life to live, too. The customers will turn to someone else because of necessity, but if you did a good job for them and were reliable in the past and being there when you were supposed to be, they will surely call you again. (When you get to this stage, you can classify it one of two ways—either you've reached your independence or you're totally burned out!)

—Customers call you back again and again.

—Your customers ask you to hold their keys for future visits. This is a good feeling, because you know they trust you.

—Your customers tell others about you. It is a good feeling when someone calls, and tells you that someone referred them to you.

—You decide to refuse a customer, even if they're willing to pay triple the money. (This doesn't happen often.) I believe an explanation is appropriate. You remembered this person calling before. When you told them your rate, they laughed at you (not a snicker, but a full-belly laugh!) and said they could get a neighborhood boy to do it for a buck. So, you know they must have gotten that boy the last time. Did something go wrong? (Perhaps he forgot; perhaps he decided to have a party in the house; perhaps the pet got out; perhaps he isn't available this time.) Whatever the reason you're suddenly worth the money, you don't know what it is, and you honestly don't care. Some people may see this as being vindictive—you're just not fond of discourteous people.

THE ANSWERS TO THE QUESTIONS I'M SURE YOU ARE ASKING:

Are the incidents in these CHAPTERs all true?

Yes, they are.

Why did I decide to print the book in black and white?

To prove a point…just as there is an obvious, undeniable, and unmistakable difference between these two colors—the same is true of pet sitters. Either you are the type of person to become a professional and successful sitter or you're not. There are Professional Pet Sitters, and then there are those who are just sitting for extra pocket money. The difference shows in a sitter's telephone etiquette, how they present themselves when they go to meet a customer, how they care for the pet(s), how willing they are to go the extra mile when unexpected things happen, how quickly the pet(s) warm up to them (when a person truly adores animals, the animals can sense it) . Most importantly, a Professional Pet Sitter is committed—when they say they will be there for a pet, they will be there. It's their job.

There is also an undeniable difference between hiring a Professional Pet Sitter, and kenneling your pet(s).

Am I still pet sitting?

Yes, I am still pet sitting. I am able to do so because I have an exceptionally understanding and loving husband (I am sure it is obvious to you now as to why I dedicated this book to him!), no small children, a true love for animals... and to be shamelessly honest, I am perfect for this job. I have always worked best independently, and am very self-motivated. Do I ever get tired or burned out? Yes. Do I ever get tired of picking up poohs? Yes. Do I ever get tired of dogs wanting their behinds scratched? No!

Even though some exasperating things have happened to me in my years as a Professional Pet Sitter. . . and even though I am not making the money I could make in an office. . .and even though I don't get any paid sick or vacation days—I have never once said that I would do things differently, if I could go back in time...*I AM HAPPIER.*

CONCLUSION

Just before finishing this book, I was contacted by a local news reporter. The paper was searching for different and exciting feature stories. I felt as though I was dreaming, and told myself I'd believe this when I see it. A reporter was sent to interview me, and took several pictures of me with one of my clients' dogs. It was then that I realized this could really happen! They wouldn't waste all this film on me, if they weren't serious! Two weeks later a full-page article was done; they included one large picture. Needless to say, I was ecstatic. After eight years, I was finally getting some recognition!

The first inquiry generated from that article was for the care of a full-grown pot belly pig. Asked if I had ever taken care of a pig before, I answered honestly—I hadn't. The owner was also honest, informing me that some people are a little afraid of "Anna Belle", because she sometimes chews at your feet to try to intimidate you. I decided I'd wear leather shoes, and wasn't too concerned. My rate was included in the article, and I just went with that. I went to meet "Anna Belle" and her owners. Almost immediately, "Anna Belle" greeted me, and started to chew my shoe. Since they had warned me, I just stood there, and didn't budge. When she realized I wasn't afraid of her, she calmly walked away. I was then told that she was usually free to roam the kitchen, porch, and other areas of the house. I was then in awe as they showed me how she sits and gives you her hoof on command. They also told me how they need to keep a lock on the refrigerator. Then they took it off, and showed me how she comes to tell them the lock isn't on, as if to say "if you don't lock it, I'm going in!". She would have access only to the porch and the yard while they were away. I was told that, since she is a white pig they put sunscreen on her to keep her from burning (I wasn't asked to do this.) I was given instructions on how to feed her. That night I was picturing myself going there, and leaving with no shoes… and perhaps no toes! The first day she greeted me at the gate. I had taken the food with me, so that I could give her an apple when I first came in the gate. She knew I had the rest of her food in a bag, swallowed the apple whole, and followed me to the porch. Not giving me time to go in first to put her food in her bowl, she proceeded to try to get through the open storm door right along side of me! There we were, stuck side by side! The whole time I could picture myself stuck there until someone came to free us. Finally, she freed herself, and I found that I was stuck on the door's spring, which was broken and hanging there. My sweatshirt somehow got tangled in it. "Anna Belle" was making all kinds of noises… she was hungry, and wanted her food. It took me a while, but I was able to free myself. From then on it was smooth snouting…I mean sailing…next time I knew to leave her apple and carrot at the gate, and rush to put her meal and water in the porch. Everything went fine after that. I decided "Anna Belle" is a very sweet animal, and can now understand why they would want her around. I actually gave them a credit, and lowered their rate for future visits! (Competitors, beware! I'm hard to compete with!) Also, since I've reached adulthood, I haven't consumed much meat—now for sure I'll be telling them to "hold the ham".

So, there you have it—the truth, the whole truth, and nothing but the truth.

For those of you who have never heard about pet sitting before—I am happy that you now know that there are other options besides transporting your pets to a kennel. They really are much happier in their own environment. When returning home from their travels, many of our clients tell us "they feel bad, because it doesn't seem like their pet(s) even missed them"!

To those of you who are potential sitters—quite simply, if you have the required attributes, a strong will, someone to lean on, a little luck, plenty of determination, you're not afraid of commitment, and you are prepared for anything—you will succeed as a Professional Pet Sitter.

GOOD LUCK!

If you need help with forms, business cards, etc., please E-mail NOAH'S ARK PET SERVICES at NOAHS_ARK_SITTING@ BLACKBOARD.COM. We will advise you as to how we can be of help.

SUZANNE M. ROTH